MODERN RUSSIAN MASTERWORKS

SERGEI PROKOFIEV

SONATA OPUS 94
FOR VIOLIN AND PIANO

In the summer of 1943, Sergei Prokofiev (1891-1953) completed his Sonata in D for Flute and Piano, Op. 94, a piece in Classical style, written when the composer was also working on the music for "Ivan the Terrible." The Sonata received its first public performance in Moscow on December 7, 1943, with Nikolai Kharkovsky, flute, and Sviatoslav Richter, piano.

Prokofiev transcribed the flute part for violin in 1944. This version was first performed by David Oistrakh, violin, and Lev Oborin, piano, on June 17, 1944. Later the piece was published as the Sonata No. 2 for Violin and Piano, Op. 94 *bis*.

The present edition has been thoroughly edited and contains both the flute and violin versions in the piano score. The variations between the two versions in regard to tempo and technique can be clearly distinguished.

ISBN 978-1-4234-5507-3

G. SCHIRMER, *Inc.*

DISTRIBUTED BY

HAL•LEONARD®
CORPORATION

7777 W. BLUEMOUND RD. P.O. BOX 13819 MILWAUKEE, WI 53213

www.schirmer.com
www.halleonard.com

SONATA

For Flute or Violin and Piano

New Revised Version

Sergei Prokofiev
Op. 94

I

II
(Scherzo)

22

MODERN RUSSIAN MASTERWORKS

SERGEI PROKOFIEV

SONATA OPUS 94
FOR VIOLIN AND PIANO

VIOLIN PART

ISBN 978-1-4234-5507-3

G. SCHIRMER, *Inc.*

DISTRIBUTED BY

HAL•LEONARD®
CORPORATION
7777 W. BLUEMOUND RD. P.O. BOX 13819 MILWAUKEE, WI 53213

www.schirmer.com
www.halleonard.com

In the summer of 1943, Sergei Prokofiev (1891-1953) completed his Sonata in D for Flute and Piano, Op. 94, a piece in Classical style, written when the composer was also working on the music for "Ivan the Terrible." The Sonata received its first public performance in Moscow on December 7, 1943, with Nikolai Kharkovsky, flute, and Sviatoslav Richter, piano.

Prokofiev transcribed the flute part for violin in 1944. This version was first performed by David Oistrakh, violin, and Lev Oborin, piano, on June 17, 1944. Later the piece was published as the Sonata No. 2 for Violin and Piano, Op. 94 *bis*.

The present edition has been thoroughly edited and contains both the flute and violin versions in the piano score. The variations between the two versions in regard to tempo and technique can be clearly distinguished.

SONATA
For Flute or Violin and Piano

Violin Version

I

Sergei Prokofiev
Op. 94

4

6

II
(Scherzo)

III

IV

18

III

IV